CW00519641

Keto Diet

Cookbook

Meat Recipes

Boost Your Health with Fast and Easy Air Fryer Recipes Affordable for Beginners.

Celine Cunningham

Table of Contents

Introduction

What is Keto Diet?

Keto diet (Ketogenic diet) this is a low-carb diet with a high percentage of fat in the diet, in which the body produces ketones in the liver and uses them as energy.

Initially the main most familiar and accessible source of energy for our body is glucose. When you eat something high in carbohydrates, our body processes them into glucose, which increases the blood sugar and for its stabilization and the distribution of glucose in the cells of the body, the pancreas produces insulin.

Glucose is the simplest molecule in our body that is converted and used as energy, so it will be chosen over any other source of energy.

Insulin is produced to process glucose in the blood by moving it throughout the body.

Since glucose is used as an energy source, your fats are not needed and therefore accumulate. Typically, in a normal, higher carbohydrate diet, the body will use glucose as the main form of energy. By reducing carbohydrate intake, the body is induced into a condition known as ketosis.

Ketosis is a natural condition of our body, which starts with a low content of glucose in the diet. With him, the body produces ketones, splitting fatty acids, to provide us with a sufficient level of energy, nutrition of brain cells and organs.

The main goal and ultimate goal of keto diets is to switch us to the state of ketosis. It is important to understand that it does not start with a lowcalorie

intake, but with a low carbohydrate content in the diet.

Our bodies are incredibly adaptive - as soon as they lack glucose, they easily switch to ketosis and begin to use fats as the main source of energy.

The optimal level of ketones and low blood sugar levels give us a lot of advantages: from a general improvement in health and a decrease in the percentage of subcutaneous fat, to an increase in mental concentration, energy level and vitality.

A keto-diet implies a high fat content, a moderate protein content and a very low carbohydrate content.

Nutrient intake should be about 70% fat, 25% protein and 5% carbohydrates.

What Keto Can Do For You

Keto has its origins in treating healthcare conditions such as epilepsy, type 2

diabetes, cardiovascular disease, metabolic syndrome, auto-brewery

syndrome and high blood pressure but now has much wider application in

weight control.

This diet, then, will take you above and beyond typical results and propel

youinto a new realm of total body health. If you want to look and feel the

best youpossibly can, all without sacrificing your love of delicious food, then

this is thecookbook for you.

Why are people going on the ketogenic diet even if they don't have

epilepsy? As the keto diet became a more popular alternative to fasting,

people began noticing additional benefits, like weight loss. Here are the

most reported benefits of the low-carb, high-fat diet:

Cutting out lots of carbs can lead to weight loss

Significantly restricting carbs causes the body to produce ketones, but it also

prevents excess glucose from getting stored as body fat. Lots of people who

go on the keto diet find that losing weight is much easier. This is especially

true if your current diet is high in refined, simple carbs like white bread,

pasta, and sugar. Carbs are not inherently evil - as we mentioned before,

the body actually needs them - but refined carbs are not very nutritious and

usually end up stored as fat. When you eliminate them, weight loss is more

likely.

The diet improves energy levels

You probably are familiar with the sluggish feeling after eating a carb-heavy meal. That's because your body is working so hard to process the carbs. You get an initial burst of energy and then a crash. When you cut out those refined carbs and instead eat foods higher in fat, that fatigue goes away. Your blood sugar levels become more stabilized throughout the day instead of going on a rollercoaster. The high-fat diet also helps with mental energy, since the brain is especially fond of fats found in coconut oil and fatty fish.

Your skin and hair health improve

A lot of people who go on the keto diet report having healthier skin, hair, and even fingernails. Fat is a hydrating nutrient, and hair and skin love it. Hair becomes shinier, sleeker, and less brittle. Skin also becomes healthier and less dry, while cutting out inflammatory foods like sugar can help clear up acne.

The keto diet might prevent certain diseases

There isn't a ton of research into the keto diet's effect on disease, but early studies are intriguing. Heart disease is a top killer, especially in the United States, and the keto diet can help people maintain better blood pressure. A high body mass is linked to heart disease, so losing weight thanks to the keto diet can also protect a person from the disease. The keto diet's effect on the brain is also significant, and studies have shown that ketones might help prevent and even treat brain disorders like Alzheimer's.

The Keto Flu and how to avoid it.

Keto flu is not a virus that infects only those who decide to try a ketogenic diet. This is the body's response to carbohydrate restriction.

The most common symptoms of keto-flu are craving for sugar, dizziness, irritability, fog in the head and poor concentration, stomach pain, nausea, cramps, muscle soreness and insomnia.

To avoid this, follow these simple rules:

1. Drink more water (with a pinch of unrefined salt).

Hydration is vital, especially when you are on a ketogenic diet. If during a keto diet you do not drink enough water, you can easily dehydrate and experience side effects.

2. Supplement your diet with sodium, potassium and magnesium.

To get enough potassium, add avocados and leafy greens such as spinach to your diet. Add a little crude salt to each meal and to water to replenish sodium levels.

Magnesium is another important mineral that can significantly ease your transition to ketosis. Although you do not lose magnesium, while limiting carbohydrates, it is important to help you prevent and eliminate cramps, improve sleep quality and increase insulin sensitivity. Simply add pumpkin seeds, almonds and spinach to your diet.

3. Eat more fat.

To help your body adapt, eat more fat. Fat provides Acetyl-CoA liver cells, which they can use to make ketones.

4. In the morning, do exercises with low intensity.

When you wake up, fill the bottle with water and a pinch of salt, and go for a walk. The walk should be at a pace where you can easily talk without gasping. It is desirable to walk about an hour.

As you continue walking, you should feel better and better and more and more awake. This is a form of low intensity exercise that will help increase fat burning, and you will not have to suffer from keto flu.

5. Relieve stress through meditation.

When you start a ketogenic diet, you may be tenser and more irritable than usual. This is due to the fact that your cortisol levels are slightly higher than usual.

To help reduce cortisol levels and improve overall well-being, it is best to do daily meditation.

Every day, for 15 minutes, just sit silently, inhaling and exhaling slowly and deeply.

The purpose of meditation is not to be thoughtless, so as not to be distracted by the thought, but to concentrate on breathing. This is how you train your mind so that life is less stressful.

6. A good sleep is the key to success.

Another way to reduce stress levels is to ensure good sleep. Good sleep is especially important for ketogenic diets. Without this, cortisol levels will increase, which complicates keto-flu and keto-adaptation. Sleep at least 7-9 hours every night, and if you feel tired in the middle of the day, lie down for 30 minutes or meditate.

To fall asleep faster at night, turn off all lights (including the phone) at least 30 minutes before you go to bed. This will help you translate your mind from work mode to sleep mode.

1. Tasty Roasted Pork Belly

Preparation time: 10 minutes **Cooking time:** 1 hour and 30 minutes **Servings:**

6

Ingredients:

- 2 tbsp. stevia
- 1 tbsp. lemon juice
- 1 quart water
- 17 ounces apples, cored and cut into wedges
- 2 pounds pork belly, scored
- Salt and black pepper to the taste
- A drizzle of olive oil

Instructions:

1. In your blender, mix water with apples, lemon juice and stevia and pulse very well.

2. Put the pork belly in a steamer tray and steam for 1 hour.

3. Transfer pork belly to a baking sheet, rub with a drizzle of oil, season with salt and pepper and pour the apple sauce over it.

4. Introduce in the oven at 425 degrees F for 30 minutes.

5. Slice pork roast, divide between plates and serve with the applesauce on top.

Nutrition: cal.456, fat 34, fiber 4, carbs 10, protein 25

2. Stuffed Pork

Preparation time: 10 minutes **Cooking time:** 30 minutes **Servings:** 4

Ingredients:

- Zest of 2 limes
- Zest from 1 orange
- Juice from 1 orange
- Juice from 2 limes
- 4 tsp. garlic, minced
- ¾ cup olive oil
- 1 cup cilantro, chopped
- 1 cup mint, chopped
- 1 tsp. oregano, dried
- Salt and black pepper to the taste
- 2 tsp. cumin, ground
- 4 pork loin steaks
- 2 pickles, chopped
- 4 ham slices
- 6 Swiss cheese slices
- 2 tbsp. mustard

Instructions:

1. In your food processor, mix lime zest and juice with orange

zest and juice, garlic, oil, cilantro, mint, oregano, cumin, salt and pepper and blend well.

2. Season steaks with salt and pepper, place them into a bowl, add marinade you've made, toss to coat and leave aside for a couple of hours.

3. Place steaks on a working surface, divide pickles, cheese, mustard and ham on them, roll and secure with toothpicks.

4. Heat up a pan over medium high heat, add pork rolls, cook them for 2 minutes on each side and transfer them to a baking sheet.

5. Introduce in the oven at 350 degrees F and bake for 25 minutes.

6. Divide between plates and serve.

Nutrition: cal.270, fat 7, fiber 2, carbs 3, protein 20

3. **Pork Chops**

Preparation time: 10 minutes **Cooking time:** 40 minutes **Servings:** 3

Ingredients:

- 8 ounces mushrooms, sliced
- 1 tsp. garlic powder
- 1 yellow onion, chopped
- 1 cup mayonnaise
- 3 pork chops, boneless
- 1 tsp. nutmeg
- 1 tbsp. balsamic vinegar
- ½ cup coconut oil

Instructions:

1. Heat up a pan with the oil over medium heat, add mushrooms and onions, stir and cook for 4 minutes.

2. Add pork chops, season with nutmeg and garlic powder and brown on both sides.

3. Introduce pan in the oven at 350 degrees F and bake for 30 minutes.

4. Transfer pork chops to plates and keeps warm.

5. Heat up the pan over medium heat, add vinegar and mayo over mushrooms mix, stir well and take off heat.

Nutrition: cal.600, fat 10, fiber 1, carbs 8, protein 30

4. <u>Italian Pork Rolls</u>

Preparation time: 10 minutes **Cooking time:** 20 minutes **Servings:** 6

Ingredients:

- 6 prosciutto slices
- 2 tbsp. parsley, chopped
- 1 pound pork cutlets, thinly sliced
- 1/3 cup ricotta cheese
- 1 tbsp. coconut oil
- ¼ cup yellow onion, chopped
- 3 garlic cloves, minced
- 2 tbsp. parmesan, grated

- 15 ounces canned tomatoes, chopped
- 1/3 cup chicken stock
- Salt and black pepper to the taste
- ½ tsp. Italian seasoning

Instructions:

1. Use a meat pounder to flatten pork pieces.

2. Place prosciutto slices on top of each piece, then divide ricotta, parsley and parmesan.

3. Roll each pork piece and secure with a toothpick.

4. Heat up a pan with the oil over medium heat, add pork rolls, cook until they are brown on both sides and transfer to a plate.

5. Heat up the pan again over medium heat, add garlic and onion, stir and cook for 5 minutes.

6. Add stock and cook for 3 minutes more.

7. Discard toothpicks from pork rolls and return them to the pan.

8. Add tomatoes, Italian seasoning, salt and pepper, stir, bring to a boil, reduce heat to medium-low, cover pan and cook for 30 minutes. Divide between plates and serve.

Nutrition: cal.280, fat 17, fiber 1, carbs 2, protein 34

5. Lemon And Garlic Pork

Preparation time: 10 minutes **Cooking time:** 30 minutes **Servings:** 4

Ingredients:

- 3 tbsp. ghee
- 4 pork steaks, bone in
- 1 cup chicken stock
- Salt and black pepper to the taste
- A pinch of lemon pepper
- 3 tbsp. coconut oil
- 6 garlic cloves, minced
- 2 tbsp. parsley, chopped
- 8 ounces mushrooms, roughly chopped
- 1 lemon, sliced

Instructions:

1. Heat up a pan with 2 tbsp. ghee and 2 tbsp. oil over medium high heat, add pork steaks, season with salt and pepper, cook until they are brown on both sides and transfer to a plate.

2. Return pan to medium heat, add the rest of the ghee and oil and half of the stock.

3. Stir well and cook for 1 minute.

4. Add mushrooms and garlic, stir and cook for 4 minutes.

5. Add lemon slices, the rest of the stock, salt, pepper and lemonpepper, stir and cook everything for 5 minutes.

6. Return pork steaks to pan and cook everything for 10 minutes more.

7. Divide steaks and sauce between plates and serve.

Nutrition: cal.456, fat 25, fiber 1, carbs 6, protein 40

6. <u>Tasty and Smoked Beef Mélange</u>

Preparation Time: 1 hour 40 minutes | Servings 6

- **Ingredients:**
- 2 pounds cubed boneless beef sirloin steak
- 3 tsp.s tallow at room temperature
- 1/2 tsp. crushed black peppercorns
- Cayenne pepper and seasoned salt to taste
- 2 cloves minced garlic
- 1 tsp. crushed caraway seeds
- 1/2 tsp. mustard seeds
- 1 tbsp. smoked paprika
- 1 cup chopped yellow onions
- 1 rosemary sprig
- 2 thyme sprigs
- 6 cups bone broth
- 1 tbsp. fish sauce
- 1 tbsp. dry white wine
- 2 bay leaves
- 2 pureed ripe Roma tomatoes

Instructions:

1. In a heavy-bottomed pan heat 1 tsp. of the tallow over a medium heat. Fry the beef until it goes from pink to brown.

2. Season with cayenne pepper, black peppercorns and salt. Take the beef out of the pan.

3. Put in the other 2 tsp.s of tallow in the pan and melt over a medium heat. Sauté the garlic and onions until they are soft. Keep stirring the whole time.

4. Add the thyme, rosemary, mustard seeds, caraway seeds and paprika. Cook for 1 minute until they are aromatic. 5. Add the bone broth, fish sauce, white wine, bay leaves and tomatoes. Partially cover and cook for 1 and a half hours. Get rid of the bay leaves and put the beef into individual bowls. Bon appétit!

Nutrition: Calories 375 ;Protein 55.1g ;Fat 13.3g ;Carbs 5.6g ;Sugars 2.9g

7. <u>Beef Soup with a Drizzle of Chili</u>

Preparation Time: 1 hour 10 minutes | Servings 6

Ingredients:

- 2 pounds cubed and boneless well-marbled beef chuck
- 1 tbsp. canola oil
- 2 chopped carrots
- 1 chopped celery with leaves
- 1 chopped parsnip
- 2 peeled and chopped onions
- 1/2 cup pitted and halved ripe olives

- 6 cups of water
- 2 tbsp.s instant bouillon granules
- 1 pureed ripe tomato
- 1/2 tsp. ground cumin
- 1/2 tsp. ground bay leaf
- 1/2 cup frozen green peas
- **For the drizzle of chili:**
- 1 tbsp. extra-virgin olive oil
- 2 red chilies
- Salt, to taste
- 2 tbsp.s lemon juice

Instructions:

1. In a stockpot heat the canola oil over a medium-high heat. Cook the beef cubes for 3 to 5 minutes until they are brown. Take the beef out of the pot.

2. Cook the carrots, celery, parsnip and onions in the pan drippings until they are tender. Add the water, bouillon granules, olives, tomato, cumin and bay leaves.

3. Stir in the beef cubes and bring the soup to the boil.

4. Partially cover the stockpot and simmer the soup for 50 minutes at medium low. Add the green peas and simmer for an additional 15 minutes.

5. While this is cooking, make the chili drizzle. Blend the olive oil, chilies, lemon juice and salt in a food processor.

6. Pour the soup into individual bowls and top with the chili drizzle.

Nutrition: Calories 375 Protein 14.4g, Fat 47.6g ; Carbs

4.8g ;Protein 47.6g ;Sugars 1.7g

8. <u>Rich Beef Hotchpotch</u>

Preparation Time: 2 hours | Servings 4

Ingredients:

- 1 1/2 pounds ground beef
- 2 tbsp.s lard
- 2 minced garlic cloves
- 1 stick of chopped celery
- 1 finely minced jalapeno pepper
- 2 chopped bell peppers
- 1 chopped carrot
- 2 chopped leeks
- 4 cups beef broth
- Pepper and salt, to taste
- 1 tsp. fennel seeds
- 1 tsp. dried marjoram
- 1 tbsp. flaxseed meal
- 1/4 tsp. freshly grated nutmeg

Instructions:

1. In a pan Dutch oven melt 1 tbsp. of lard. Crumble the beef with a

spatula while browning it in the fat. Then take the beef out of the pan Dutch

oven.

2. Melt the rest of the lard in the pan Dutch oven and cook the garlic cloves,

celery, pepper, carrot and leeks until they are soft.

3. Put the beef back in to the pan Dutch oven and pour the beef broth over it. Add the pepper, salt, fennel seeds and marjoram. Bring to the boil.

4. Simmer the mixture on a medium-low heat for about an hour and 50 minutes.

5. Stir in the flaxseed meal and boil for a couple of minutes stirring most of the time. Sprinkle the nutmeg on top and serve in individual bowls.

Nutrition: Calories 467 Protein 58g ; Fat 18.7g ; Carbs 3.7g ; Sugars 1.2g

9. <u>Burger Soup with Cheese and Vinegar</u>

Preparation Time: 30 minutes | Servings 6

Ingredients:

- 1 1/2 pounds ground chuck
- 1 tbsp. olive oil
- 2 chopped garlic cloves
- 2 chopped onions
- 1 cup pureed ripe tomatoes
- 2 cups bone broth
- Ground black peppercorns and salt to taste
- 1 tsp. dried oregano
- 2 bay leaves

- 1 cup shredded Colby cheese
- 2 tbsp.s ume plum vinegar

Instructions:

1. In a pot, heat the oil over a medium heat. Fry the beef until it has browned, crumbling it with a fork all the time. Take the beef out of the pot, drain and put to one side.

2. Fry the garlic and onions in the pan drippings and cook for around 5 minutes or until they are soft.

3. Add the pureed ripe tomatoes, bone broth, oregano, bay leaves, pepper and salt. Bring to the boil and cook for another 20 minutes.

4. Sprinkle in the Colby cheese and cook until the cheese has melted.

5. Pour into individual soup bowls. Drizzle the soup with ume plum vinegar and serve hot. Bon appétit!

Nutrition: Calories 238 Protein 25.1g ;Fat 12.6g ; 5.6g

Carbs; 2.5g Sugars

10. <u>Beef Ribs with Marsala Wine</u>

Preparation Time: 2 hours 30 minutes | Servings 8

Ingredients:

- 2 pounds beef ribs
- 1/4 tsp. ground black pepper
- 1/4 tsp. kosher salt
- 1 tbsp. coconut oil
- 1/2 cup Marsala wine
- 2 tsp. chili powder
- 2 minced garlic cloves
- 3/4 cup pureed fresh ripe tomatoes

Instructions:

1. Put your oven on at 325 degrees F.

2. Season the beef ribs all over with chili powder, black pepper and salt.

3. In a large skillet heat the coconut oil over a medium-high heat. Flash-fry the beef ribs until they are brown all over. Put the ribs in a casserole dish.

4. In a mixing bowl, combine the Marsala wine, chili powder, garlic cloves and pureed tomatoes. Pour this mixture over the beef ribs.

5. Put a piece of foil over the dish. Leave the ribs to roast in the oven for 2 hours. Roast for another 20 to 30 minutes without the foil.

Nutrition: Calories 231 Protein 8.9 g, Fat 34.7g ; ;Carbs 1.3g ;Sugars 0.7g

11. Spicy Ground Beef Sauerkraut Casserole

Preparation Time: 20 minutes | Servings 4

Ingredients:

- 2 minced garlic cloves
- 2 chopped onions,
- 1 1/4 pounds ground beef
- 1 tbsp. melted tallow
- 18 ounces rinsed and drained sauerkraut
- 1 bay leaf
- 1 tsp. chili pepper flakes
- 1 tsp. mustard powder

- Ground black pepper and sea salt, to taste

Instructions:

1. Put a saucepan over a medium-high heat. Warm the tallow and sauté the garlic and onions until fragrant.

2. Put in the ground beef and fry until it is fairly brown.

3. Add the sauerkraut, bay leaf, chili pepper flakes, mustard powder, pepper and salt. Turn the heat down to medium and cook for about 6 minutes until everything is cooked through. Bon appétit!

Nutrition: Calories 330 Protein 12.2g, Fat 44.4g ;Carbs 4.7g ;Sugars 2.6g

12.   <u>Winter Cheeseburger Soup</u>

Preparation Time: 20 minutes | Servings 4

Ingredients:

- 1/2 pound ground beef
- 1 cup chopped shallots
- 1 tbsp. chopped celery leaves
- 1 chopped celery stalk

- 2 tbsp.s coconut oil
- 1 tbsp. chopped fresh cilantro
- 4 cups beef bone broth
- 1/2 cup full-fat milk
- 1 tbsp. rice vinegar
- 1 cup shredded pepper jack cheese

Instructions:

1. In a stock pot heat the coconut oil over a medium heat. Brown the ground beef and take out of the pot.

2. Add the celery stalk and shallots. Cook for another 2 minutes, stirring all the time. If needed add a little broth.

3. Put in the cilantro, celery leaves and broth. Bring to the boil, partially cover the pot and cook for another 10 minutes.

4. Add the milk slowly to the soup, while stirring. Turn down the heat and simmer for an additional 5 minutes. Sprinkle in the cheese and take the pot off the heat.

5. Keep stirring until the cheese has melted and add the vinegar. Bon appétit!

Nutrition: Calories 326 Protein 26.8g ; Fat 20.5 g ;Carbs 4.5g ;Sugars 1.6g

13.   Zucchini Spaghetti Bolognese

Preparation Time: 1 hour 35 minutes | Servings 4

Ingredients:

For Bolognese:

- 1 finely chopped carrot
- 1 finely chopped celery with leaves
- 1 finely chopped onion
- 2 thinly sliced garlic cloves
- 2 tbsp.s olive oil
- 1 pound ground beef
- 2 chopped slices of bacon
- 2 tbsp.s tomato paste
- 2 pureed tomatoes
- 1/2 cup water
- 1/2 cup dry white wine
- 2 rosemary sprigs
- 1 tsp. fresh thyme leaves
- 1 tsp. dried oregano
- 1 tsp. dried basil
- Ground black pepper and salt, to taste

For Zucchini Spaghetti:

- 2 tbsp.s olive oil
- 4 peeled zucchinis

- 1/4 cup water
- Salt, to taste

Instructions:

1. Preheat a sauté pan over a medium flame and heat 1 tbsp. of the olive oil. Sauté the carrots, celery, garlic and onions until they are fairly soft.

2. Add the ground beef and the bacon and cook for 7 minutes. Break any lumps with a spatula.

3. Stir in the tomato paste, tomatoes, wine, rosemary, thyme, oregano, basil, pepper and salt. Simmer over a medium-low heat for 1 and a quarter hours. Modify the seasoning if needed.

4. While this is cooking. make your zucchini spaghetti. Slice the zucchinis into noodle-shaped strands.

5. In a pan heat the other tbsp. of oil over a moderate heat for a minute, stirring all the time. Cook for another 6 minutes after adding water.

6. Sprinkle the zucchini with salt and serve with the Bolognese sauce.

Nutrition: Calories 477 Protein 25.6g Fat 41.8g ;Carbs 6.3g ; Sugars 4.3g

14. Filet Mignon and Sour Cream Sauce

Preparation Time: 20 minutes | Servings 4

Ingredients:

- 4 1 1/2 inch thick filet mignon steaks
- 1 1/2 tbsp.s finely chopped flat-leaf parsley
- 1 tbsp. stone-ground mustard
- 1/3 cup sour cream
- 1/4 tsp. ground black pepper
- 1/2 tsp. seasoned salt
- 1 sprig chopped rosemary

- 2 springs chopped thyme
- 1 tbsp. vegetable oil

Instructions:

1. Whisk together the parsley, sour cream and mustard in a bowl. Put into the

refrigerator.

2. Season the filet mignon steaks with rosemary, thyme, pepper and salt.

3. Preheat a pan over a medium-high heat and heat the oil. Cook the steaks

for 4 minutes on each side. Serve with the sour cream and mustard sauce and

Nutrition: Calories 321 Protein 13.7g, Fat 45g ; Carbs 1g ;Protein 45g ;Sugars

0g

15. **Cheeky Beef Short Loin**

Preparation Time: 2 hours | Servings 4

Ingredients:

- 1 pound thinly sliced beef short loin
- 1 tbsp. olive oil
- 3 thinly sliced garlic cloves
- 1 sliced leek
- 1 chopped parsnip
- 1 tsp. lemon zest
- 1/2 tsp. grated nutmeg
- 1/2 tsp. crushed red pepper flakes
- 1 1/2 cups beef stock
- 3 cups red wine
- 2 tbsp.s Worcestershire sauce

Instructions:

1. Preheat a heavy-bottomed skillet and heat the oil over a medium heat. Sear the beef for between 10 and 13 minutes. Take out of the skillet.

2. Put the parsnip, garlic and leeks in the skillet and cook for 3 to 4 minutes. Stir continually. Add the lemon zest, nutmeg, red pepper flakes, beef stock, red wine and the Worcestershire sauce and bring to a rapid boil. Then, simmer for 1 and a half to 2 hours. Bon appétit!

Nutrition: Calories 238 Protein 9.2g, Fat 27.4g ;Carbs 6.3g ;Sugars 2.7g

16. Jamaican Pork

Preparation time: 10 minutes **Cooking time:** 45 minutes **Servings:** 12

Ingredients:

- 4 pounds pork shoulder
- 1 tbsp. coconut oil
- ½ cup beef stock
- ¼ cup Jamaican jerk spice mix

Instructions:

1. Rub pork shoulder with Jamaican mix and place in your instant pot.

2. Add oil to the pot and set it to Sauté mode.

3. Add pork shoulder and brown it on all sides.

4. Add stock, cover pot and cook on High for 45 minutes.

5. Uncover pot, transfer pork to a platter, shred and serve.

Nutrition: cal.267, fat 20, fiber 0, carbs 0, protein 24

17.   <u>Cranberry Pork Roast</u>

Preparation time: 10 minutes **Cooking time:** 8 hours **Servings:** 4

Ingredients:

- 1 tbsp. coconut flour
- Salt and black pepper to the taste
- 1 and ½ pounds pork loin
- A pinch of mustard, ground

- ½ tsp. ginger
- 2 tbsp. sukrin
- 2 tbsp. sukrin gold
- ½ cup cranberries
- 2 garlic cloves, minced
- ½ lemon sliced
- ¼ cup water

Instructions:

1. In a bowl, mix ginger with mustard, salt, pepper and flour and stir.

2. Add roast, toss to coat and transfer meat to a Crockpot.

3. Add sukrin and sukrin gold, cranberries, garlic, water and lemon slices.

4. Cover pot and cook on Low for 8 hours.

5. Divide on plates, drizzle pan juices on top and serve.

Nutrition: cal.430, fat 23, fiber 2, carbs 3, protein 45

18. Juicy Pork Chops

Preparation time: 10 minutes **Cooking time:** 45 minutes **Servings:** 4

Ingredients:

- 2 yellow onions, chopped
- 6 bacon slices, chopped
- ½ cup chicken stock
- Salt and black pepper to the taste
- 4 pork chops

Instructions:

1. Heat up a pan over medium heat, add bacon, stir, cook until it's crispy and transfer to a bowl.

2. Return pan to medium heat, add onions, some salt and pepper, stir, cover, cook for 15 minutes and transfer to the same bowlwith the bacon.

3. Return pan once again to heat, increase to medium high, add pork chops, season with salt and pepper, brown for 3 minutes on one side, flip, reduce heat to medium and cook for 7 minutes more.

4. Add stock, stir and cook for 2 minutes more.

5. Return bacon and onions to the pan, stir, cook for 1 minute more, divide between plates and serve.

Nutrition: cal.325, fat 18, fiber 1, carbs 6, protein 36

19. **<u>Simple And Fast Pork Chops</u>**

Preparation time: 10 minutes **Cooking time:** 15 minutes **Servings:** 4

Ingredients:

- 4 medium pork loin chops
- 1 tsp. Dijon mustard
- 1 tbsp. Worcestershire sauce
- 1 tsp. lemon juice
- 1 tbsp. water
- Salt and black pepper to the taste
- 1 tsp. lemon pepper
- 1 tbsp. ghee
- 1 tbsp. chives, chopped

Instructions:

1. In a bowl, mix water with Worcestershire sauce, mustard and lemon juice and whisk well.

2. Heat up a pan with the ghee over medium heat, add pork chops, season with salt, pepper and lemon pepper, cook them for 6 minutes, flip and cook for 6 more minutes.

3. Transfer pork chops to a platter and keep them warm for now.

4. Heat up the pan again, pour mustard sauce you've made andbring to a gentle simmer.

5. Pour this over pork, sprinkle chives and serve.

Nutrition: cal.132, fat 5, fiber 1, carbs 1, protein 18

20. **Mediterranean Pork**

Preparation time: 10 minutes **Cooking time:** 35 minutes **Servings:** 4

Ingredients:

- 4 pork chops, bone-in
- Salt and black pepper to the taste
- 1 tsp. rosemary, dried
- 3 garlic cloves, minced

Instructions:

1. Season pork chops with salt and pepper and place in a roasting pan.

2. Add rosemary and garlic, introduce in the oven at 425 degrees F and bake for 10 minutes.

3. Reduce heat to 350 degrees F and roast for 25 minutes more.

4. Slice pork, divide between plates and drizzle pan juices all over.

Nutrition: cal.165, fat 2, fiber 1, carbs 2, protein 26

21. Pork Chops Delight

Preparation time: 10 minutes **Cooking time:** 40 minutes **Servings:** 4

Ingredients:

- 4 pork chops
- 1 tbsp. oregano, chopped
- 2 garlic cloves, minced
- 1 tbsp. canola oil
- 15 ounces canned tomatoes, chopped
- 1 tbsp. tomato paste
- Salt and black pepper to the taste
- ¼ cup tomato juice

Instructions:

1. Heat up a pan with the oil over medium high heat, add pork chops, season with salt and pepper, cook for 3 minutes, flip, cook for 3 minutes more and transfer to a plate.

2. Return pan to medium heat, add garlic, stir and cook for 10 seconds.

3. Add tomato juice, tomatoes and tomato paste, stir, bring to a boil and reduce heat to medium-low.

4. Add pork chops, stir, cover pan and simmer everything for 30

minutes.

5. Transfer pork chops to plates, add oregano to the pan, stir and

cook for 2 minutes more.

6. Pour this over pork and serve.

Nutrition: cal.210, fat 10, fiber 2, carbs 6, protein 19

22. <u>Stuffed Zucchini with pork and mushrooms</u>

Preparation Time: 50 minutes | Servings 8

Ingredients:

- 2 tbsp.s canola oil
- 4 halved medium-sized zucchinis
- 1 pound ground pork
- 2 chopped shallots
- 1 pressed garlic clove
- 1 cup chopped button mushrooms
- 2 pureed tomatoes
- 1/2 cup chicken stock

- Ground black pepper and salt, to taste
- 1 cup freshly grated Colby cheese

Instructions:

1. Put your oven on at 360 degrees F. Spray a baking pan with nonstick cooking spray.

2. Scoop out the zucchini flesh.

3. In a saucepan heat the oil over a medium flame. Sweat the shallots for around 3 minutes. Stir constantly.

4. Add the garlic and cook for 1 minute. Put in the mushrooms and ground pork. Cook for another 5 minutes.

5. Add the chicken stock and pureed tomatoes. Season with pepper and salt, to taste.

6. Turn down the flame to a moderate heat. Partially cover the pan and simmer for 10 minutes. Stir every now and then.

7. Put the mixture in the zucchini halves. Place them in the baking tray and cook for around 27 minutes. Sprinkle the freshly grated cheese on top and serve hot. Bon appétit!

Nutrition: Calories 230;Protein 23.2g, Fat 11.8g ;Carbs 5.5g

;Sugars 2.2g

23.   Rustic Pork Goulash and Cauliflower Rice

Preparation Time: 25 minutes | Servings 6

- **Ingredients:**
- 1 heaped tsp. garlic paste
- 2 chopped white onions
- 1 tbsp. lard at room temperature
- 2 slices chopped bacon
- $\frac{1}{4}$ pound ground pork
- Red pepper and salt, to taste
- 1 1/2 cups bone broth
- 1 tsp. capers
- 2 ripe Roma tomatoes
- 1 bay leaf
- 2 tsp.s fennel seeds
- 2 tsp.s smoked cayenne pepper
- 1/2 cup loosely packed and roughly chopped fresh cilantro
- 2 cups cooked cauliflower rice

Instructions:

1. Preheat a pan over a medium high heat. Melt the lard. Sauté the garlic and onions under just soft and aromatic.

2. Add the ground pork, and cook for 7 minutes, crumbling with a fork. Add the capers, bacon, red pepper and salt. Cook for another 2 minutes.

3. Add the broth, fennel seeds, tomatoes, bay leaf and cayenne pepper. Turn down the heat to medium-low. Simmer until it is all cooked through; it should take 10 - 13 minutes.

4. Decorate with fresh cilantro and serve with hot cauliflower rice.

Nutrition: Calories 228 ;Protein 8.7g, Fat 30.1g ; Carbs

5.8g ;Protein 30.1g ;Sugars 2.6g

24. Classic Pork Stew and Steamed Broccoli

Preparation Time: 2 hours | Servings 6

Ingredients:

- 2 tbsp.s lard at room temperature
- 1 tsp. paprika
- Ground black pepper, to taste
- 1 1/2 pounds cubed pork stewing meat
- 1 tsp. finely minced garlic
- 1 chopped leek
- 1/4 cup dry red wine
- 1/2 tsp. celery seeds
- 2 bay leaves

- 1 tbsp. beef bouillon granules
- 3 cups water
- 1 stalk chopped celery
- 2 chopped bell peppers
- 1 chopped habanero pepper
- 1 tbsp. flax seed meal
- 1 tbsp. chopped fresh coriander
- 1 cup broccoli florets

Instructions:

1. Rub the pork with paprika and black pepper.

2. Preheat a stockpot over a high flame and melt the lard. Cook the pork for about 8 minutes until brown. Stir now and then. Take out of the pot and keep warm.

3. Sauté the garlic and leeks for 8 to 9 minutes in the pan drippings until they are soft. Scrape up any brown bits in the pot by adding a splash of red wine.

4. Add the wine, celery seeds, bay leaves, beef bouillon granules, water, celery, bell peppers, the habanero pepper and coriander. Cover the pot and put the heat on medium-low. Simmer for 1 and three quarter hours.

5. Put in the flax seed meal and cook for 4 minutes, stirring continuously.

6. While this is cooking fill a large pan with 1-inch of water. Bring to the boil.

Put a steamer basket inside the pan and cook the broccoli until tender. This should take around 9 minutes.

7. Season the broccoli with salt and serve with the warm pork stew.

Nutrition: Calories 336 Protein 15.9g, Fat 35g ; Carbs 6g ;Sugars 2.1g

25. <u>Mom's Special Pork Stew</u>

Preparation Time: 25 minutes | Servings 4

Ingredients:

- 3/4 pound cubed boneless pork shoulder
- 1 tsp. deveined and minced habanero pepper
- 2 chopped shallots
- 1 chopped carrot
- 1 tbsp. butter
- 1 1/2 cups bone broth
- 2 tbsp.s garlic paste
- 1/2 tsp. ground cloves
- 1/2 tsp. ground bay leaf
- 1 tbsp. chopped fresh parsley
- Ground black pepper and Himalayan salt
- 1 pitted, peeled and diced avocado
- 1/2 cup full-fat sour cream

Instructions:

1. Preheat a heavy-bottom pot over a medium heat and melt the butter.

2. Sauté the carrot, habanero pepper and shallots until they are tender; about 3 minutes.

3. Add the cubed pork and cook for a further 5 minutes, stirring often.

4. Add the bay leaf, cloves, broth, garlic paste, salt and pepper. Turn up the heat to medium-high and bring it to the boil.

5. Reduce the heat to a simmer and cook an extra 15 minutes or until thoroughly heated.

6. Put the mixture in to individual dishes. On top of each dish sprinkle the parsley and add the avocado and sour cream.

Nutrition: Calories 295 Protein 20.3g ;Fat 19.6g ;Carbs 4.7g ;Sugars 1.6g

26. **Pork Meatballs and Herb Sauce**

Preparation Time: 50 minutes | Servings 6

Ingredients:

For the Meatballs:

- 1 ground pound pork
- 1/4 cup almond flour
- 3/4 cup grated parmesan cheese1
- 1 beaten egg
- 2 ounces full-fat milk
- Ground black pepper and salt, to taste
- 1 tsp. garlic paste
- 1 finely chopped white onion
- 1 tsp. onion flakes
- 2 tbsp.s chili powder
- 2 tbsp.s chopped fresh parsley

For the Sauce:

- 2 chopped ripe tomatoes
- 2 tbsp.s olive oil
- Ground black pepper and salt, to taste
- 1 tsp. garlic
- 1 tsp. crushed red pepper flakes
- 1 thyme sprig
- 1 rosemary sprig

- 1 tbsp. cider vinegar

Instructions:

1. Put your oven on at 360 degrees F. Spray an oven dish with a nonstick cooking spray.

2. In a mixing dish bowl combine the pork, almond flour, parmesan, egg, milk, pepper, salt, garlic paste, onion, onion flakes, chili powder and parsley. Form the mixture into 2-inch balls and place them in the baking dish in a single layer. Spray the meatballs with the cooking spray.

3. In another mixing bowl combine the tomatoes, olive oil, pepper, salt, garlic, red pepper flakes, thyme, rosemary and cider vinegar. Pour the tomato sauce over the meatballs.

4. Bake until everything is heated through; about 45 minutes. Bon appétit!

Nutrition: Calories 237 Protein 26.4g ;Fat 12g, Carbs 5.6g

;Protein 26.4g ;Sugars 2.7g

27. <u>Wholesome Pork Soup with Parsley</u>

Preparation Time: 20 minutes | Servings 6

Ingredients:

- 1 1/4 pounds chunks of pork shoulder
- 2 tbsp.s lard
- 1 chopped celery
- 1 medium peeled and chopped yellow onion

- 2 peeled and minced cloves of garlic
- 1 tsp. Mezzeta pepper
- 3 cups low-sodium beef broth
- Ground black pepper and sea salt, to taste
- 2 ripe undrained tomatoes
- A pinch of dried basil
- 1 medium pitted, peeled and sliced avocado
- 1/4 fresh roughly chopped parsley

Instructions:

1. In a large stockpot melt the lard over a medium flame. Sauté the garlic, celery, Mezzeta pepper and onion until the onion is transparent; about 2 to 3 minutes.

2. Put the pork chunks in the stockpot and carry on cooking for another 4 minutes, stirring all the time. Add the broth, pepper, salt, tomatoes and basil.

3. Partially cover the pot. Lower the heat and simmer for 10 minutes. Stir every now and then.

4. Serve topped with the sliced avocado and the fresh parsley leaves.

Nutrition: Calories 423 Protein 25.9g ;Fat 31.8g ;Carbs 6g

;Sugars 2.9g

28.   Greek Souvlaki with a Side of Tzatziki

Preparation Time: 20 minutes + marinating time | Servings 6

Ingredients:

- 1 tsp. Greek oregano
- 3 smashed cloves garlic
- 2 tbsp.s chopped cilantro
- 2 tbsp.s fresh lemon juice
- 1/3 cup red wine vinegar
- Ground black pepper and sea salt, to taste
- 2 pounds cubed pork loin, trimmed of silver skin and excess fat
- Wooden skewers, soaked in cold water for half an hour before use

For Tzatziki Sauce:

- 1 cup full-fat Greek yogurt
- 1 small shredded and drained cucumber
- 3 tsp.s olive oil
- 1 tsp. smashed garlic
- Sea salt, to taste
- 2 tsp.s finely minced fresh dill

Instructions:

1. Make the marinade first. To make the marinade, thoroughly combine the Greek oregano, garlic, cilantro, lemon juice, red wine vinegar, pepper and salt.

2. Cover the pork loin with the marinade. Put it in the refrigerator and leave for 3 hours. When this is ready thread the pork cubes onto the skewers.

3. Grill your souvlaki, browning them all over. This should take 8 to 12 minutes.

4. Mix the yogurt, cucumber, olive oil, garlic, salt and dill to make the tzatziki sauce. Serve the tzatziki with souvlaki skewers. Bon appétit!

Nutrition: Calories 147 ;Protein 17.3g ;Fat 4.8g ; Carbs

6.2g ;Sugars 5.5g

29. **Meatloaf from Kansas City**

Preparation Time: 1 hour 10 minutes | Servings 8

Ingredients:

- 2 pounds ground pork
- 1/2 cup chopped shallots
- 1/2 cup bottle chipotle salsa
- 2 beaten eggs
- 8 ounces shredded sharp Cheddar cheese
- 1 tsp. paprika
- 1 tsp. garlic powder
- Freshly ground black pepper and sea salt, to taste
- 1 tbsp. whole grain mustard

- 1 tsp. lime zest
- 1/2 cup tomato paste
- 1 tbsp. Swerve

Instructions:

1. Put your oven on at 360 degrees F.

2. In a bowl combine the ground pork with the eggs, cheese, shallots, paprika, garlic powder, pepper, salt, mustard and lime zest.

3. Mix until everything is well integrated. Grease a loaf pan with nonstick cooking spray and put the pork mixture into the loaf pan.

4. Whisk together the Swerve with the tomato paste. Put this mixture on top of the loaf.

5. Cook for about 65 minutes, rotating the pan once or twice. If you wish you can place it under the broiler for the last 5 minutes of cooking time.

6. The meatloaf needs to stand for 5 to 10 minutes before slicing.

Nutrition: Calories 318 ;Protein 39.3g ;Fat 14.7g ;Carbs 6.2g ;Sugars 2.4g

30. <u>Sassy Pork Indian-Style</u>

Preparation Time: 1 hour 15 minutes | Servings 8

Ingredients:

- 2 pounds cubed pork belly
- 1 tbsp. olive oil
- Freshly ground pepper and salt
- 2 minced garlic cloves
- 2 tsp.s ground coriander
- A bunch of chopped scallions
- 1/2 tbsp. ground cloves
- 1/2 tbsp. curry powder
- 1 deveined and chopped bell pepper
- 2 pureed tomatoes
- 1/2 tsp. fennel seeds
- 1 deveined and minced Thai chili
- 2 cups bone broth
- 1/2 cup unsweetened coconut milk

Instructions:

1. In a saucepan heat the oil over a medium heat. Sprinkle the pork belly with pepper, salt and ground coriander.

2. Cook the pork for about 10 minutes. Stir often and then remove.

3. Next, cook the garlic, scallions, cloves and curry powder in the pan drippings. Put the mixture in the slow cooker. Add the bell pepper, tomatoes, fennel seeds, Thai chili, bone broth, and coconut milk. Cover the slow cooker and cook on a low heat for 1 hour.

Nutrition: Calories 369 ;Protein 41.3g, Fat 20.2g ;Carbs 2.9g ;Protein 41.3g ;Sugars 1.5g

31. Marinated Pork Rib Chops with Spinach

Preparation Time: 25 minutes + marinating time | Servings 6

Ingredients:

- 1 1/2 pounds pork rib chops
- Ground black pepper and sea salt, to taste
- 1 tbsp. garlic paste
- $\frac{1}{4}$ cup Champagne wine
- 2 tbsp.s oyster sauce
- 1 tbsp. cider vinegar
- 1 tbsp. fresh lime juice
- 2 tsp.s olive oil
- 1 chopped bell pepper
- 1 sliced red onion
- 1 sliced celery stalk
- 2 cups spinach

Instructions:

1. Rub the pork rib chops with pepper and salt. In a small bowl, whisk together the garlic paste, Champagne wine, oyster sauce, cider vinegar and fresh lime juice.

2. Put the marinade on the pork and let it stand for around 2 hours.

3. Preheat a large pan over a medium heat and heat up 1 tsp. of the olive oil. Cook the bell pepper, onion and celery for about 5 minutes. Stir often and then take out of the pan.

4. Heat the other tsp. of olive oil in the same pan. Put the pork in with the marinade. Brown the pork for between 3 and 5 minutes each side.

5. Add the vegetables to the pan together with the spinach. Cook for about 6 minutes until the spinach leaves are wilted. Serve warm. Bon appétit!

Nutrition: Calories 234 ;Protein 29.8g ;Fat 11g ; Carbs 2g ;Sugars 0.6g

32. <u>Spicy Pork Chops</u>

Preparation time: 4 hours and 10 minutes **Cooking time:** 15 minutes

Servings:4

Ingredients:

- ¼ cup lime juice
- 4 pork rib chops
- 1 tbsp. coconut oil, melted

- 2 garlic cloves, minced
- 1 tbsp. chili powder
- 1 tsp. cinnamon, ground
- 2 tsp. cumin, ground
- Salt and black pepper to the taste
- ½ tsp. hot pepper sauce
- Sliced mango for serving

Instructions:

1. In a bowl, mix lime juice with oil, garlic, cumin, cinnamon, chili powder, salt, pepper and hot pepper sauce and whisk well.

2. Add pork chops, toss to coat and leave aside in the fridge for 4 hours.

3. Place pork on preheated grill over medium heat, cook for 7 minutes, flip and cook for 7 minutes more.

4. Divide between plates and serve with mango slices on the side.

Nutrition: cal.200, fat 8, fiber 1, carbs 3, protein 26

33. Tasty Thai Beef

Preparation time: 10 minutes **Cooking time:** 10 minutes **Servings:** 6

Ingredients:

- 1 cup beef stock
- 4 tbsp. peanut butter
- ¼ tsp. garlic powder
- ¼ tsp. onion powder
- 1 tbsp. coconut aminos
- 1 and ½ tsp. lemon pepper
- 1 pound beef steak, cut into strips
- Salt and black pepper to the taste
- 1 green bell pepper, chopped
- 3 green onions, chopped

Instructions:

1. In a bowl, mix peanut butter with stock, aminos and lemon pepper, stir well and leave aside.

2. Heat up a pan over medium high heat, add beef, season with salt, pepper, onion and garlic powder and cook for 7 minutes. Add green pepper, stir and cook for 3 minutes more.

4. Add peanut sauce you've made at the beginning and green onions, stir, cook for 1 minute more, divide between plates and serve.

Nutrition: cal.224, fat 15, fiber 1, carbs 3, protein 19

34. **The Best Beef Patties**

Preparation time: 10 minutes **Cooking time:** 35 minutes **Servings:** 6

Ingredients

- ½ cup bread crumbs
- 1 egg
- Salt and black pepper to the taste
- 1 and ½ pounds beef, ground
- 10 ounces canned onion soup
- 1 tbsp. coconut flour
- ¼ cup ketchup

- 3 tsp. Worcestershire sauce
- ½ tsp. mustard powder
- ¼ cup water

Instructions:

1. In a bowl, mix 1/3 cup onion soup with beef, salt, pepper, egg and bread crumbs and stir well.

2. Heat up a pan over medium high heat, shape 6 patties from the beef mix, place them into the pan and brown on both sides.

3. Meanwhile, in a bowl, mix the rest of the soup with coconut flour, water, mustard powder, Worcestershire sauce and ketchup and stir well.

4. Pour this over beef patties, cover pan and cook for 20 minutes stirring from time to time.

5. Divide between plates and serve.

Nutrition: cal.332, fat 18, fiber 1, carbs 7, protein 25

35. <u>Amazing Beef Roast</u>

Preparation time: 10 minutes **Cooking time:** 1 hour and 15 minutes

Servings: 4

Ingredients:

- 3 and ½ pounds beef roast
- 4 ounces mushrooms, sliced
- 12 ounces beef stock
- 1 ounce onion soup mix
- ½ cup Italian dressing

Instructions:

1. In a bowl, mix stock with onion soup mix and Italian dressing and stir.

2. Put beef roast in a pan, add mushrooms, stock mix, cover with tin foil, introduce in the oven at 300 degrees F and bake for 1 hour and 15 minutes.

3. Leave roast to cool down a bit, slice and serve with the gravy on top.

Nutrition: cal.700, fat 56, fiber 2, carbs 10, protein 70

36. Ground Beef Casserole

Preparation time: 10 minutes **Cooking time:** 35 minutes **Servings:** 6

Ingredients:

- 2 tsp. onion flakes
- 1 tbsp. gluten free Worcestershire sauce
- 2 pounds beef, ground
- 2 garlic cloves, minced
- Salt and black pepper to the taste
- 1 cup mozzarella cheese, shredded
- 2 cups cheddar cheese, shredded
- 1 cup Russian dressing
- 2 tbsp. sesame seeds, toasted

- 20 dill pickle slices
- 1 romaine lettuce head, torn

Instructions:

1. Heat up a pan over medium heat, add beef, onion flakes,

Worcestershire sauce, salt, pepper and garlic, stir and cook for

5 minutes.

2. Transfer this to a baking dish, add 1 cup cheddar cheese over it

and also the mozzarella and half of the Russian dressing.

3. Stir and spread evenly.

4. Arrange pickle slices on top, sprinkle the rest of the cheddar

and the sesame seeds, introduce in the oven at 350 degrees f

and bake for 20 minutes.

5. Turn oven to broil and broil the casserole for 5 minutes more.

6. Divide lettuce on plates, top with a beef casserole and the rest

of the Russian dressing.

Nutrition: cal.554, fat 51, fiber 3, carbs 5, protein 45

37. <u>**Zoodles And Beef**</u>

Preparation time: 10 minutes **Cooking time:** 20 minutes **Servings:** 5

Ingredients:

- 1 pound beef, ground
- 1 yellow onion, chopped
- 2 garlic cloves, minced
- 14 ounces canned tomatoes, chopped
- 1 tbsp. rosemary, dried
- 1 tbsp. sage, dried
- 1 tbsp. oregano, dried
- 1 tbsp. basil, dried
- 1 tbsp. marjoram, dried
- Salt and black pepper to the taste
- 2 zucchinis, cut with a spiralizer

Instructions:

1. Heat up a pan over medium heat, add garlic and onion, stir and brown for a couple of minutes.

2. Add beef, stir and cook for 6 minutes more.

3. Add tomatoes, salt, pepper, rosemary, sage, oregano, marjoram and basil, stir and simmer for 15 minutes. Divide zoodles into bowls, add beef mix and serve.

Nutrition: cal.320, fat 13, fiber 4, carbs 12, protein 40

38. **Jamaican Beef Pies**

Preparation time: 10 minutes **Cooking time:** 35 minutes **Servings:** 12

Ingredients:

- 3 garlic cloves, minced
- ½ pound beef, ground
- ½ pound pork, ground
- ½ cup water
- 1 small onion, chopped
- 2 habanero peppers, chopped
- 1 tsp. Jamaican curry powder
- 1 tsp. thyme, dried
- 2 tsp. coriander, ground

- ½ tsp. allspice
- 2 tsp. cumin, ground
- ½ tsp. turmeric
- A pinch of cloves, ground
- Salt and black pepper to the taste
- 1 tsp. garlic powder
- ¼ tsp. stevia powder
- 2 tbsp. ghee
- *For the crust:*
- 4 tbsp. ghee, melted
- 6 ounces cream cheese
- A pinch of salt
- 1 tsp. turmeric
- ¼ tsp. stevia
- ½ tsp. baking powder
- 1 and ½ cups flax meal
- 2 tbsp. water
- ½ cup coconut flour

Instructions:

1. In your blender, mix onion with habaneros, garlic and ½ cup water.

2. Heat up a pan over medium heat, add pork and beef meat, stir and cook for 3 minutes.

3. Add onions mix, stir and cook for 2 minutes more.

4. Add garlic, onion, curry powder, ½ tsp. turmeric, thyme, coriander, cumin, allspice, cloves, salt, pepper, stevia powder and garlic powder, stir well and cook for 3 minutes.

5. Add 2 tbsp. ghee, stir until it melts and take this off heat.

6. Meanwhile, in a bowl, mix 1 tsp. turmeric, with ¼ tsp. stevia, baking powder, flax meal and coconut flour and stir.

7. In a separate bowl, mix 4 tbsp. ghee with 2 tbsp. water and cream cheese and stir.

8. Combine the 2 mixtures and mix until you obtain a dough.

9. Shape 12 balls from this mix, place them on a parchment paper and roll each into a circle.

10. Divide beef and pork mix on one half of the dough circles, cover with the other halves, seal edges and arrange them all on a lined baking sheet.

11. Bake your pies in the oven at 350 degrees F for 25 minutes.

12. Serve them warm.

Nutrition: cal.267, fat 23, fiber 1, carbs 3, protein 12

39. **Amazing Goulash**

Preparation time: 10 minutes **Cooking time:** 20 minutes **Servings:** 5

Ingredients:

- 2 ounces bell pepper, chopped
- 1 and ½ pounds beef, ground
- Salt and black pepper to the taste
- 2 cups cauliflower florets
- ¼ cup onion, chopped
- 14 ounces canned tomatoes and their juice
- ¼ tsp. garlic powder
- 1 tbsp. tomato paste
- 14 ounces water

Instructions:

1. Heat up a pan over medium heat, add beef, stir and brown for 5 minutes.

2. Add onion and bell pepper, stir and cook for 4 minutes more.

3. Add cauliflower, tomatoes and their juice and water, stir, bring to a simmer, cover pan and cook for 5 minutes.

4. Add tomato paste, garlic powder, salt and pepper, stir, take off heat, divide into bowls and serve.

Nutrition: cal.275, fat 7, fiber 2, carbs 4, protein 10

40. __Beef And Eggplant Casserole__

Preparation time: 30 minutes **Cooking time:** 4 hours **Servings:** 12

Ingredients:

- 1 tbsp. olive oil
- 2 pounds beef, ground
- 2 cups eggplant, chopped
- Salt and black pepper to the taste
- 2 tsp. mustard
- 2 tsp. gluten free Worcestershire sauce
- 28 ounces canned tomatoes, chopped

- 2 cups mozzarella, grated
- 16 ounces tomato sauce
- 2 tbsp. parsley, chopped
- 1 tsp. oregano, dried

Instructions:

1. Season eggplant pieces with salt and pepper, leave them aside for 30 minutes, squeeze water a bit, put them into a bowl, add the olive oil and toss them to coat.

2. In another bowl, mix beef with salt, pepper, mustard and Worcestershire sauce and stir well.

3. Press them on the bottom of a crock pot.

4. Add eggplant and spread.

5. Also add tomatoes, tomato sauce, parsley, oregano and mozzarella.

6. Cover Crockpot and cook on Low for 4 hours.

7. Divide casserole between plates and serve hot.

Nutrition: cal.200, fat 12, fiber 2, carbs 6, protein 15

41. **Braised Lamb Chops**

Preparation time: 10 minutes **Cooking time:** 2 hours and 20 minutes

Servings: 4

Ingredients:

- 8 lamb chops
- 1 tsp. garlic powder
- Salt and black pepper to the taste
- 2 tsp. mint, crushed
- A drizzle of olive oil
- 1 shallot, chopped
- 1 cup white wine
- Juice of ½ lemon
- 1 bay leaf
- 2 cups beef stock
- Some chopped parsley for serving
- *For the sauce:*
- 2 cups cranberries
- ½ tsp. rosemary, chopped
- ½ cup swerve
- 1 tsp. mint, dried
- Juice of ½ lemon
- 1 tsp. ginger, grated
- 1 cup water
- 1 tsp. harissa paste

Instructions:

1. In a bowl, mix lamb chops with salt, pepper, 1 tsp. garlic powder and 2 tsp. mint and rub well.

2. Heat up a pan with a drizzle of oil over medium high heat, add lamb chops, brown them on all sides and transfer to a plate.

3. Heat up the same pan again over medium high heat, add shallots, stir and cook for 1 minute.

4. Add wine and bay leaf, stir and cook for 4 minutes.

5. Add 2 cups beef stock, parsley and juice from ½ lemon, stir and simmer for 5 minutes.

6. Return lamb, stir and cook for 10 minutes.

7. Cover pan and introduce it in the oven at 350 degrees F for 2 hours.

8. Meanwhile, heat up a pan over medium high heat, add cranberries, swerve, rosemary, 1 tsp. mint, juice from ½ lemon, ginger, water and harissa paste, stir, bring to a simmer for 15 minutes.

9. Take lamb chops out of the oven, divide them between plates, drizzle the cranberry sauce over them and serve.

Nutrition: cal.450, fat 34, fiber 2, carbs 6, protein 26

42. <u>**Lamb Salad**</u>

Preparation time: 10 minutes **Cooking time:** 35 minutes **Servings:** 4

Ingredients:

- 1 tbsp. olive oil
- 3 pounds leg of lamb, bone discarded and butterflied
- Salt and black pepper to the taste
- 1 tsp. cumin, ground
- A pinch of thyme, dried
- 2 garlic cloves, minced
- *For the salad:*
- 4 ounces feta cheese, crumbled
- ½ cup pecans

- 2 cups spinach
- 1 and ½ tbsp. lemon juice
- ¼ cup olive oil
- 1 cup mint, chopped

Instructions:

1. Rub lamb with salt, pepper, 1 tbsp. oil, thyme, cumin and minced garlic, place on preheated grill over medium high heat and cook for 40 minutes, flipping once.

2. Meanwhile, spread pecans on a lined baking sheet, introduce in the oven at 350 degrees F and toast for 10 minutes.

3. Transfer grilled lamb to a cutting board, leave aside to cool down and slice.

4. In a salad bowl, mix spinach with 1 cup mint, feta cheese, ¼ cup olive oil, lemon juice, toasted pecans, salt and pepper and toss to coat.

5. Add lamb slices on top and serve.

Nutrition: cal.334, fat 33, fiber 3, carbs 5, protein 7

43. **Moroccan Lamb**

Preparation time: 10 minutes **Cooking time:** 15 minutes **Servings:** 4

Ingredients:

- 2 tsp. paprika
- 2 garlic cloves, minced
- 2 tsp. oregano, dried
- 2 tbsp. sumac
- 12 lamb cutlets
- ¼ cup olive oil
- 2 tbsp. water
- 2 tsp. cumin, ground
- 4 carrots, sliced
- ¼ cup parsley, chopped

- 2 tsp. harissa
- 1 tbsp. red wine vinegar
- Salt and black pepper to the taste
- 2 tbsp. black olives, pitted and sliced
- 6 radishes, thinly sliced

Instructions:

1. In a bowl, mix cutlets with paprika, garlic, oregano, sumac, salt, pepper, half of the oil and the water and rub well.

2. Put carrots in a pot, add water to cover, bring to a boil over medium high heat, cook for 2 minutes drain and put them in a salad bowl.

3. Add olives and radishes over carrots.

4. In another bowl, mix harissa with the rest of the oil, parsley, cumin, vinegar and a splash of water and stir well.

5. Add this to carrots mix, season with salt and pepper and toss to coat.

6. Heat up a kitchen grill over medium high heat, add lamb cutlets, grill them for 3 minutes on each side and divide them between plates.

7. Add carrots salad on the side and serve.

Nutrition: cal.245, fat 32, fiber 6, carbs 4, protein 34

44. <u>**Delicious Lamb And Mustard Sauce**</u>

Preparation time: 10 minutes **Cooking time:** 20 minutes **Servings:** 4

Ingredients:

- 2 tbsp. olive oil
- 1 tbsp. fresh rosemary, chopped
- 2 garlic cloves, minced
- 1 and ½ pounds lamb chops
- Salt and black pepper to the taste
- 1 tbsp. shallot, chopped
- 2/3 cup heavy cream
- ½ cup beef stock
- 1 tbsp. mustard
- 2 tsp. gluten free Worcestershire sauce
- 2 tsp. lemon juice
- 1 tsp. erythritol
- 2 tbsp. ghee
- A spring of rosemary
- A spring of thyme

Instructions:

1. In a bowl, mix 1 tbsp. oil with garlic, salt, pepper and rosemary and whisk well.

2. Add lamb chops, toss to coat and leave aside for a few minutes.

3. Heat up a pan with the rest of the oil over medium high heat, add lamb chops, reduce heat to medium, cook them for 7 minutes, flip, cook them for 7 minutes more, transfer to a plate and keep them warm.

4. Return pan to medium heat, add shallots, stir and cook for 3 minutes.

5. Add stock, stir and cook for 1 minute.

6. Add Worcestershire sauce, mustard, erythritol, cream, rosemary and thyme spring, stir and cook for 8 minutes.

7. Add lemon juice, salt, pepper and the ghee, discard rosemary and thyme, stir well and take off heat.

8. Divide lamb chops on plates, drizzle the sauce over them and serve.

Nutrition: cal.435, fat 30, fiber 4, carbs 5, protein 32

45. <u>Delicious Lamb Curry</u>

Preparation time: 10 minutes **Cooking time:** 4 hours **Servings:** 6

Ingredients:

- 2 tbsp. ginger, grated
- 2 garlic cloves, minced
- 2 tsp. cardamom
- 1 red onion, chopped

- 6 cloves
- 1 pound lamb meat, cubed
- 2 tsp. cumin powder
- 1 tsp. garama masala
- ½ tsp. chili powder
- 1 tsp. turmeric
- 2 tsp. coriander, ground
- 1 pound spinach
- 14 ounces canned tomatoes, chopped

Instructions:

1. In your slow cooker, mix lamb with spinach, tomatoes, ginger, garlic, onion, cardamom, cloves, cumin, garam masala, chili, turmeric and coriander, stir, cover and cook on High for 4 hours.

2. Uncover slow cooker, stir your chili, divide into bowls and serve.

Nutrition: cal.160, fat 6, fiber 3, carbs 7, protein 20

46.   Lamb Stew

Preparation time: 10 minutes **Cooking time:** 3 hours **Servings:** 4

Ingredients:

- 1 yellow onion, chopped
- 3 carrots, chopped
- 2 pounds lamb, cubed
- 1 tomato, chopped
- 1 garlic clove, minced
- 2 tbsp. ghee
- 1 cup beef stock
- 1 cup white wine
- Salt and black pepper to the taste

- 2 rosemary springs
- 1 tsp. thyme, chopped

Instructions:

1. Heat up a Dutch oven over medium high heat, add oil and heat up.

2. Add lamb, salt and pepper, brown on all sides and transfer to a plate.

3. Add onion to the pot and cook for 2 minutes.

4. Add carrots, tomato, garlic, ghee, stick, wine, salt, pepper, rosemary and thyme, stir and cook for a couple of minutes.

5. Return lamb to pot, stir, reduce heat to medium low, cover and cook for 4 hours.

6. Discard rosemary springs, add more salt and pepper, stir, divide into bowls and serve.

Nutrition: cal.700, fat 43, fiber 6, carbs 10, protein 67

47. <u>Lamb Casserole</u>

Preparation time: 10 minutes **Cooking:** 1 hour and 40 minutes **Servings:** 2

Ingredients:

- 2 garlic cloves, minced
- 1 red onion, chopped
- 1 tbsp. olive oil
- 1 celery stick, chopped
- 10 ounces lamb fillet, cut into medium pieces
- Salt and black pepper to the taste
- 1 and ¼ cups lamb stock
- 2 carrots, chopped
- ½ tbsp. rosemary, chopped
- 1 leek, chopped
- 1 tbsp. mint sauce
- 1 tsp. stevia
- 1 tbsp. tomato puree
- ½ cauliflower, florets separated
- ½ celeriac, chopped
- 2 tbsp. ghee

Instructions:

1. Heat up a pot with the oil over medium heat, add garlic, onion and celery, stir and cook for 5 minutes.

2. Add lamb pieces, stir and cook for 3 minutes.

3. Add carrot, leek, rosemary, stock, tomato puree, mint sauce and stevia, stir, bring to a boil, cover and cook for 1 hour and 30 minutes.

4. Heat up a pot with water over medium heat, add celeriac, cover and simmer for 10 minutes.

5. Add cauliflower florets, cook for 15 minutes, drain everything and mix with salt, pepper and ghee.

6. Mash using a potato masher and divide mash between plates.

7. Add lamb and veggies mix on top and serve.

Nutrition: cal.324, fat 4, fiber 5, carbs 8, protein 20

48. <u>Amazing Lamb</u>

Preparation time: 10 minutes **Cooking time:** 8 hours **Servings:** 6

Ingredients:

- 2 pounds lamb leg
- Salt and black pepper to the taste
- 1 tbsp. maple extract
- 2 tbsp. mustard
- ¼ cup olive oil
- 4 thyme spring
- 6 mint leaves
- 1 tsp. garlic, minced
- A pinch of rosemary, dried

Instructions:

1. Put the oil in your slow cooker.

2. Add lamb, salt, pepper, maple extract, mustard, rosemary and garlic, rub well, cover and cook on Low for 7 hours.

3. Add mint and thyme and cook for 1 more hour.

4. Leave lamb to cool down a bit before slicing and serving with pan juices on top.

Nutrition: cal.400, fat 34, fiber 1, carbs 3, protein 26

49. __Beef Bourguignon__

Preparation time: 3 hours and 10 minutes **Cooking time:** 5 hours and 15

minutes **Servings:** 8

Ingredients:

- 3 tbsp. olive oil
- 2 tbsp. onion, chopped

- 1 tbsp. parsley flakes
- 1 and ½ cups red wine
- 1 tsp. thyme, dried
- Salt and black pepper to the taste
- 1 bay leaf
- 1/3 cup almond flour
- 4 pounds beef, cubed
- 24 small white onions
- 8 bacon slices, chopped
- 2 garlic cloves, minced
- 1 pound mushrooms, roughly chopped

Instructions:

1. In a bowl, mix wine with olive oil, minced onion, thyme, parsley, salt, pepper and bay leaf and whisk well.

2. Add beef cubes, stir and leave aside for 3 hours.

3. Drain meat and reserve 1 cup of marinade.

4. Add flour over meat and toss to coat.

5. Heat up a pan over medium high heat, add bacon, stir and cook until it browns a bit.

6. Add onions, stir and cook for 3 minutes more.

7. Add garlic, stir, cook for 1 minute and transfer everything to a slow cooker.

8. Also add meat to the slow cooker and stir.

9. Heat up the pan with the bacon fat over medium high heat, add mushrooms and white onions, stir and sauté them for a couple of minutes.

10. Add these to the slow cooker as well, also add reserved marinade, some salt and pepper, cover and cook on High for 5 hours.

11. Divide between plates and serve.

Nutrition: cal.435, fat 16, fiber 1, carbs 7, protein 45

50. <u>Roasted Beef</u>

Preparation time: 10 minutes **Cooking time:** 8 hours **Servings:** 8

Ingredients:

- 5 pounds beef roast
- Salt and black pepper to the taste
- ½ tsp. celery salt
- 2 tsp. chili powder
- 1 tbsp. avocado oil
- 1 tbsp. sweet paprika
- A pinch of cayenne pepper
- ½ tsp. garlic powder
- ½ cup beef stock
- 1 tbsp. garlic, minced
- ¼ tsp. dry mustard

Instructions:

1. Heat up a pan with the oil over medium high heat, add beef roast and brown it on all sides.

2. In a bowl, mix paprika with chili powder, celery salt, salt, pepper, cayenne, garlic powder and mustard powder and stir.

3. Add roast, rub well and transfer it to a Crockpot.

4. Add beef stock and garlic over roast and cook on Low for 8 hours.

5. Transfer beef to a cutting board, leave it to cool down a bit, slice and divide between plates.

6. Strain juices from the pot, drizzle over meat and serve.

Nutrition: cal.180, fat 5, fiber 1, carbs 5, protein 25

51.   Beef Stew

Preparation time: 10 minutes **Cooking time:** 4 hours and 10 minutes **Servings:** 4

Ingredients:

- 8 ounces pancetta, chopped
- 4 pounds beef, cubed
- 4 garlic cloves, minced
- 2 brown onions, chopped
- 2 tbsp. olive oil
- 4 tbsp. red vinegar
- 4 cups beef stock

- 2 tbsp. tomato paste
- 2 cinnamon sticks
- 3 lemon peel strips
- A handful parsley, chopped
- 4 thyme springs
- 2 tbsp. ghee
- Salt and black pepper to the taste

Instructions:

1. Heat up a pan with the oil over medium high heat, add pancetta, onion and garlic, stir and cook for 5 minutes. Add beef, stir and cook until it browns.

2. Add vinegar, salt, pepper, stock, tomato paste, cinnamon, lemon peel, thyme and ghee, stir, cook for 3 minutes and transfer everything to your slow cooker.

3. Cover and cook on High for 4 hours.

4. Discard cinnamon, lemon peel and thyme, add parsley, stir and divide into bowls.

5. Serve hot.

Nutrition: cal.250, fat 6, fiber 1, carbs 7, protein 33

52. <u>Lavender Lamb Chops</u>

Preparation time: 10 minutes **Cooking time:** 25 minutes **Servings:** 4

Ingredients:

- 2 tbsp. rosemary, chopped
- 1 and ½ pounds lamb chops
- Salt and black pepper to the taste
- 1 tbsp. lavender, chopped
- 2 garlic cloves, minced
- 3 red oranges, cut in halves
- 2 small pieces of orange peel
- A drizzle of olive oil

- 1 tsp. ghee

Instructions:

1. In a bowl, mix lamb chops with salt, pepper, rosemary, lavender, garlic and orange peel, toss to coat and leave aside for a couple of hours.

2. Grease your kitchen grill with ghee, heat up over medium high heat, place lamb chops on it, cook for 3 minutes, flip, squeeze 1 orange half over them, cook for 3 minutes more, flip them again, cook them for 2 minutes and squeeze another orange half over them.

3. Place lamb chops on a plate and keep them warm for now..

4. Add remaining orange halves on preheated grill, cook them for 3 minutes, flip and cook them for another 3 minutes.

5. Divide lamb chops between plates, add orange halves on the side, drizzle some olive oil over them and serve.

Nutrition: cal.250, fat 5, fiber 1, carbs 5, protein 8

53. Lamb Riblets And Tasty Mint Pesto

Preparation time: 1 hour **Cooking time:** 2 hours **Servings:** 4

Ingredients:

- 1 cup parsley
- 1 cup mint
- 1 small yellow onion, roughly chopped
- 1/3 cup pistachios
- 1 tsp. lemon zest

- 5 tbsp. avocado oil
- Salt to the taste
- 2 pounds lamb riblets
- ½ onion, chopped
- 5 garlic cloves, minced
- Juice from 1 orange

Instructions:

1. In your food processor, mix parsley with mint, 1 small onion, pistachios, lemon zest, salt and avocado oil and blend very well.

2. Rub lamb with this mix, place in a bowl, cover and leave in the fridge for 1 hour.

3. Transfer lamb to a baking dish, add garlic and ½ onion to the dish as well, drizzle orange juice and bake in the oven at 250 degrees F for 2 hours.

4. Divide between plates and serve.

Nutrition: cal.200, fat 4, fiber 1, carbs 5, protein 7

54. <u>Lamb With Fennel And Figs</u>

Preparation time: 10 minutes **Cooking time:** 40 minutes **Servings:** 4

Ingredients:

- 12 ounces lamb racks
- 2 fennel bulbs, sliced
- Salt and black pepper to the taste
- 2 tbsp. olive oil
- 4 figs, cut in halves
- 1/8 cup apple cider vinegar
- 1 tbsp. swerve

Instructions:

1. In a bowl, mix fennel with figs, vinegar, swerve and oil, toss to coat well and transfer to a baking dish.

2. Season with salt and pepper, introduce in the oven at 400 degrees F and bake for 15 minutes.

3. Season lamb with salt and pepper, place into a heated pan over medium high heat and cook for a couple of minutes.

4. Add lamb to the baking dish with the fennel and figs, introduce in the oven and bake for 20 minutes more.

5. Divide everything between plates and serve.

Nutrition: cal.230, fat 3, fiber 3, carbs 5, protein 10

55.   __Baked Veal And Cabbage__

Preparation time: 10 minutes **Cooking time:** 40 minutes **Servings:** 4

Ingredients:

- 17 ounces veal, cut into cubes
- 1 cabbage, shredded
- Salt and black pepper to the taste
- 3.4 ounces ham, roughly chopped
- 1 small yellow onion, chopped
- 2 garlic cloves, minced
- 1 tbsp. ghee
- ½ cup parmesan, grated
- ½ cup sour cream

Instructions:

1. Heat up a pot with the ghee over medium high heat, add onion, stir and cook for 2 minutes.

2. Add garlic, stir and cook for 1 minute more.

3. Add ham and veal, stir and cook until they brown a bit.

4. Add cabbage, stir and cook until it softens and the meat is tender.

5. Add cream, salt, pepper and cheese, stir gently, introduce in the oven at 350 degrees F and bake for 20 minutes.

Nutrition: cal.230, fat 7, fiber 4, carbs 6, protein 29

56. __Beef Bourguignon__

Preparation time: 3 hours and 10 minutes **Cooking time:** 5 hours and 15

minutes **Servings:** 8

Ingredients:

- 3 tbsp. olive oil
- 2 tbsp. onion, chopped
- 1 tbsp. parsley flakes
- 1 and ½ cups red wine
- 1 tsp. thyme, dried
- Salt and black pepper to the taste
- 1 bay leaf
- 1/3 cup almond flour
- 4 pounds beef, cubed
- 24 small white onions
- 8 bacon slices, chopped
- 2 garlic cloves, minced
- 1 pound mushrooms, roughly chopped

Instructions:

1. In a bowl, mix wine with olive oil, minced onion, thyme,

parsley, salt, pepper and bay leaf and whisk well.

2. Add beef cubes, stir and leave aside for 3 hours.

3. Drain meat and reserve 1 cup of marinade.

4. Add flour over meat and toss to coat.

5. Heat up a pan over medium high heat, add bacon, stir and cook until it browns a bit.

6. Add onions, stir and cook for 3 minutes more.

7. Add garlic, stir, cook for 1 minute and transfer everything to a slow cooker.

8. Also add meat to the slow cooker and stir.

9. Heat up the pan with the bacon fat over medium high heat, add mushrooms and white onions, stir and sauté them for a couple of minutes.

10. Add these to the slow cooker as well, also add reserved marinade, some salt and pepper, cover and cook on High for 5 hours.

11. Divide between plates and serve.

Nutrition: cal.435, fat 16, fiber 1, carbs 7, protein 45

57. Roasted Beef

Preparation time: 10 minutes **Cooking time:** 8 hours **Servings:** 8

Ingredients:

- 5 pounds beef roast
- Salt and black pepper to the taste
- ½ tsp. celery salt
- 2 tsp. chili powder
- 1 tbsp. avocado oil
- 1 tbsp. sweet paprika
- A pinch of cayenne pepper
- ½ tsp. garlic powder
- ½ cup beef stock
- 1 tbsp. garlic, minced
- ¼ tsp. dry mustard

Instructions:

1. Heat up a pan with the oil over medium high heat, add beef roast and brown it on all sides.

2. In a bowl, mix paprika with chili powder, celery salt, salt, pepper, cayenne, garlic powder and mustard powder and stir.

3. Add roast, rub well and transfer it to a Crockpot.

4. Add beef stock and garlic over roast and cook on Low for 8 hours.

5. Transfer beef to a cutting board, leave it to cool down a bit, slice and divide between plates.

6. Strain juices from the pot, drizzle over meat and serve.

Nutrition: cal.180, fat 5, fiber 1, carbs 5, protein 25

58. Beef Stew

Preparation time: 10 minutes **Cooking time:** 4 hours and 10 minutes

Servings: 4

Ingredients:

- 8 ounces pancetta, chopped
- 4 pounds beef, cubed
- 4 garlic cloves, minced
- 2 brown onions, chopped
- 2 tbsp. olive oil
- 4 tbsp. red vinegar
- 4 cups beef stock
- 2 tbsp. tomato paste
- 2 cinnamon sticks
- 3 lemon peel strips
- A handful parsley, chopped
- 4 thyme springs
- 2 tbsp. ghee
- Salt and black pepper to the taste

Instructions:

1. Heat up a pan with the oil over medium high heat, add pancetta, onion and garlic, stir and cook for 5 minutes. Add beef, stir and cook until it browns.

2. Add vinegar, salt, pepper, stock, tomato paste, cinnamon, lemon peel, thyme and ghee, stir, cook for 3 minutes and transfer everything to your slow cooker.

3. Cover and cook on High for 4 hours.

4. Discard cinnamon, lemon peel and thyme, add parsley, stir and divide into bowls.

5. Serve hot.

Nutrition: cal.250, fat 6, fiber 1, carbs 7, protein 33

59. Pork Stew

Preparation time: 10 minutes **Cooking time:** 1 hour and 20 minutes **Servings:**

12

Ingredients:

- 2 tbsp. coconut oil
- 4 pounds pork, cubed
- Salt and black pepper to the taste
- 2 tbsp. ghee
- 3 garlic cloves, minced
- ¾ cup beef stock
- ¾ cup apple cider vinegar
- 3 carrots, chopped
- 1 cabbage head, shredded
- ½ cup green onion, chopped
- 1 cup whipping cream

Instructions:

1. Heat up a pan with the ghee and the oil over medium high heat, add pork and brown it for a few minutes on each side.

2. Add vinegar and stock, stir well and bring to a simmer.

3. Add cabbage, garlic, salt and pepper, stir, cover and cook for 1 hour.

4. Add carrots and green onions, stir and cook for 15 minutes more.

5. Add whipping cream, stir for 1 minute, divide between plates and serve.

Nutrition: cal.400, fat 25, fiber 3, carbs 6, protein 43

60. **Sausage Stew**

Preparation time: 10 minutes **Cooking time:** 20 minutes **Servings:** 9

Ingredients:

- 1 pound smoked sausage, sliced
- 1 green bell pepper, chopped
- 2 yellow onions, chopped
- Salt and black pepper to the taste
- 1 cup parsley, chopped

- 8 green onions, chopped
- ¼ cup avocado oil
- 1 cup beef stock
- 6 garlic cloves
- 28 ounces canned tomatoes, chopped
- 16 ounces okra, chopped
- 8 ounces tomato sauce
- 2 tbsp. coconut aminos
- 1 tbsp. gluten free hot sauce

Instructions:

1. Heat up a pot with the oil over medium high heat, add

sausages, stir and cook for 2 minutes.

2. Add onion, bell pepper, green onions, parsley, salt and pepper,

stir and cook for 2 minutes more.

3. Add stock, garlic, tomatoes, okra, tomato sauce, coconut aminos and hot sauce, stir, bring to a simmer and cook for 15 minutes.

4. Add more salt and pepper, stir, divide into bowls and serve.

Nutrition: cal.274, fat 20, fiber 4, carbs 7, protein 10

61. **Burgundy Beef Stew**

Preparation time: 10 minutes **Cooking time:** 3 hours **Servings:** 7

Ingredients:

- 2 pounds beef chuck roast, cubed
- 15 ounces canned tomatoes, chopped
- 4 carrots, chopped
- Salt and black pepper to the taste
- ½ pounds mushrooms, sliced
- 2 celery ribs, chopped
- 2 yellow onions, chopped
- 1 cup beef stock
- 1 tbsp. thyme, chopped
- ½ tsp. mustard powder
- 3 tbsp. almond flour
- 1 cup water

Instructions:

1. Heat up an oven proof pot over medium high heat, add beef cubes, stir and brown them for a couple of minutes on each side.

2. Add tomatoes, mushrooms, onions, carrots, celery, salt, pepper mustard, stock and thyme and stir.

3. In a bowl mix water with flour and stir well. Add this to the pot, stir well, introduce in the oven and bake at 325 degrees F for 3 hours.

4. Stir every half an hour.

5. Divide into bowls and serve.

Nutrition: cal.275, fat 13, fiber 4, carbs 7, protein 28